Mary Bowen   Liz Hocking

English World

Pupil's Book

3

MACMILLAN

Scope and Sequence

Unit Page	Title	Reading	Lexis	Speaking	Study skills (WB)
6	Welcome Unit - Revision				
1 22	In school	*The first day in school* (a recount of past events)	school subjects; *quarter to / quarter past*	Save Henry! Part 1: *That's interesting!*	dictionary skills
2 30	On the farm	*Jack and the beanstalk* (a traditional tale)	farm animals and buildings	Save Henry! Part 2: *Pear Tree Farm*	sorting into sets
3 38	People at work	*A helicopter pilot* *A hospital nurse* (information with labels and captions)	trades and professions	Save Henry! Part 3: *Here come the workmen!*	dictionary skills
46	Revision 1				
4 48	Things we use	*The American pioneers* (information and instructions)	tools and materials	Save Henry! Part 4: *A visitor*	sorting into sets: the odd one out
5 56	Sound and pictures	*Let's listen to music!* (factual information)	audio and visual technology	Save Henry! Part 5: *The competition*	dictionary skills
6 64	Winners!	*The International Games are fantastic!* (a letter)	ordinals *7th -12th* sports	Save Henry! Part 6: *At the TV studios*	sequencing
72	Revision 2				
7 74	At the station	*The city train* *Welcome home!* (poems)	railway travel	Stop, thief! Part 1: *Hello, Toby!*	dictionary skills
8 82	In the mall	*Aunt Jemima's earring* (a story)	shops in a mall	Stop, thief! Part 2: *At the supermarket*	sorting into sets: the odd one out
9 90	Street shows	*How do they do that?* (information and an interview)	street entertainers	Stop, thief! Part 3: *In the market square*	dictionary skills
98	Revision 3				
10 100	London sights	*A trip on the Thames* (information and a strip story)	famous London landmarks	Stop, thief! Part 4: *At the bridge*	matching
11 108	World festivals	*Festivals in different seasons* (information and a play)	seasons festivals	Stop, thief! Part 5: *Is that him?*	dictionary skills
12 116	Cities at night	*Buildings around the world* (factual and descriptive information)	names of cities world landmarks	Stop, thief! Part 6: *What's going on?*	sequencing
126	Revision 4				
127	Word List				

Grammar	Grammar in conversation	Listening	Phonics	Language skills (WB)	Writing
*It **was** sunny yesterday.* ***Were** the children in school?* *Yes, they **were**. No, they **weren't**.*	*What's the time now?* *It's quarter to nine.* *It's quarter past ten.*	identifying dialogues	ar *jar*	nouns are naming words	a recount of past events
*Lulu **looked** at the horse.* ***Did** the cows **live** in the barn?* *Yes, they **did**. No, they **didn't**.*	*I visited my friend.* *Did you have a good time? Yes, I did.*	listening for gist and detail in a narrative	ou *mouse*	adjectives are describing words	a traditional tale from pictures
*The helicopter is **fast**.* *The plane is **faster**.* *The sun is **hotter than** the moon.*	*How long is your hand?* *Your hand is wider than my hand.*	identifying a description	ay *play*	verbs are doing words	information with labels and captions
***Did** the women **cook**?* *Yes they **did**. No, they **didn't**.* *The girls **skipped** with a rope.*	*The boys fetched water from the river.* *They played skittles.*	sequencing; listening for gist and detail	ow *snow*	spellings: *hop hopped* *wave waved*	instructions for making a game
*There **were** three guitars.* ***Was there** a boy in the shop?* *Yes, **there was**. No **there wasn't**.*	*Can I help you?* *How much does it cost?* *It costs £100.*	matching pictures and dialogues; gist and detail	ir *first*	spellings: *big bigger* *late later* *tiny tinier*	factual information
*They **went** to the TV studios.* ***Did** they **win** first prize?* *Yes they **did**. No, they **didn't**.*	*I like reading and listening to music.* *Do you like swimming?*	identifying descriptions, gist and detail	er *painter*	adverbs tell us about verbs	a letter about sports events
*Mum **had** the tickets.* ***Did** Grandma **have** a book?* *Yes, she **did**. No, she **didn't**.*	*You must get to school on time.* *You mustn't shout.*	following a description	y *sky*	prepositions say where things are	completing a poem
*The children **saw** the thief.* ***Did** the thief **come** back?* *Yes, he **did**. No, he **didn't**.*	*We went to the new mall.* *What did you buy?* *I bought jeans and shoes.*	identifying dialogues; gist and detail	oa *boat*	spelling: *carry carried*	continuing a story
*This car is **fast**.* *This car is **faster**.* *This car is the **fastest**.*	*What are you doing?* *I'm watching a film.* *Why? Because it's good.*	sequencing	oy *boy*	pronouns are in place of nouns	completing an interview
*The cars **are going to** stop.* *What **is** the bridge **going to** do?* *It **is going to** open.*	*I'm going to have a salad.* *Would you like one?* *No, thanks. I'd like…?* *Can I have…?*	listening for gist and detail	ur *burn*	punctuating direct speech	strip story with direct speech
*There is **some** juice.* *There are **some** cakes.* *Is there **any** water?* *There aren't **any** grapes.*	*I've got some sandwiches.* *Have you got any fruit?* *I haven't got any grapes.*	sequencing; listening for detail	or *morning*	comma with *and* at the end of a list	completing a dialogue
*This hat is **mine**. This shoe is **yours**.* *This shirt is **his**. This bag is **hers**.* *These hats are **ours**.* *These boots are **theirs**.*	*What's the date today?* *It's the fifteenth of May.*	sequencing; listening for detail	ow *tower*	plurals: *baby, babies* *boy, boys* *dish dishes*	descriptive information

Say Hello to ...

Miss Carey   **Alfie**   **Lulu**   **Molly**   **Max**   **Toby**

Mr Oats

Gary West

Alan

Percy the pencil

Paddy the pencil-sharpener

Ronnie the rubber

Rosie the ruler

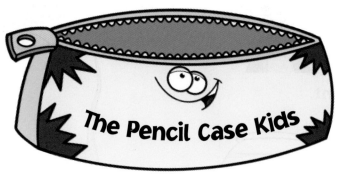

The Pencil Case Kids

Pete the paperclip

We help with Phonics.

We help with Listening.

We help with Grammar.

We help with Writing.

Welcome Unit

1  **Listen and read.**

Hello! I'm Lulu.

Hello! I'm Max.

Hi! I'm Molly.

Hi! I'm Alfie.

And I'm Miss Carey. Hello!

2 **Listen and point.**

A Who are they? Write.

1 <u>She is Miss Carey.</u>

2 _____

3 _____

4 _____

3 Ask and answer.

Who is she?

She's Lulu.

1   2

3

4 Ask and answer.

What has she got?

She's got a bird.

1   2

3

This is a doll.

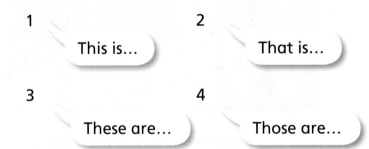

5 What are they saying?
Point to the picture and say.

1   2

This is…   That is…

3   4

These are…   Those are…

B What have they got? Write.

Remember!   He's got = He has got
                They've got = They have got

1    She has got a bird.

2  _____

3   _____

4   _____

1 🎧 Listen and read.

1

I'm reading.

She's reading.

2

We're playing football.

They're playing football.

4

They're watching TV.

5

It's flying over the sea.

7

He's walking through the trees.

8

They're sleeping.

A What are they doing? Write.

Remember! I'm = I am   He's = He is
They're = They are

1   _She is singing._

2   _____

3   _____

4 What are **you** doing?

_____

3

He's jumping into the water.

6

They're running across the bridge.

9

She's singing.

2 Ask and answer.

What's the time?

It's seven o'clock.

What's the time?

It's half past ten.

3 What are they doing?
Ask and answer.

What is she doing?

She's reading.

B Write. Complete the sentences with *over*, *through*, *across* and *into*.

1

The boy is swimming _____ the river.

2

She is walking _____ the flowers.

3

The birds are flying _____ the trees.

4

He's looking _____ the box.

1 Name the hobbies.

_____ _____ _____ _____

Alfie

Lulu

Max and Molly

We don't like te

I like football.

Look at me!

2 🎧 **Listen and say the hobbies.**

3 Now you!

A Complete the sentences with *like* or *likes*.

1 We _____ swimming.

2 Molly _____ basketball.

3 Lulu and Miss Carey _____ reading.

4 Alfie _____ football.

_____   _____

Miss Carey

Look at us!

4 Ask and answer.

Does Lulu like reading?

Yes, she does.

Do Molly and Max like tennis?

No, they don't.

1 Alfie – football?
2 Miss Carey – swimming?
3 Molly and Max – basketball?
4 Lulu – football?
5 Alfie – singing?
6 Miss Carey – reading?

5 Ask, find and answer.

Can you see the lion?

Yes, I can see it.

Use these words in your answers:

| him | her | it | them |

B Complete the sentences with *do* or *does*.

1 _____ you like reading?

2 _____ Lulu like basketball?

3 Max and Molly _____ not like tennis.

4 Alfie _____ not like singing.

1 🎧 **Listen to Joe and point to the pictures.**

2 🎧 **Listen again. Number the pictures in order.**

A **Write. Use the words in the box.**   walk   get up   play   eat

1 Joe always _____ at seven o'clock.

2 Max sometimes _____ to school.

3 Max and Molly never _____ tennis.

4 Alfie always _____ a big breakfast.

D

H

L

3 Ask and answer.

1 When does Joe get up?

2 When do you get up?

3 What does he do first?

4 Where does he eat breakfast?

5 Does he walk to school?

6 Do his friends go to school on the bus?

4 Choose *always*, *sometimes* or *never*.

I walk to school.

I sometimes walk to school.

1 I get up at six o'clock.

2 I clean my teeth.

3 I brush my hair.

4 I eat breakfast in the sitting room.

5 I go to school with my friends.

6 I go to bed at nine o'clock.

B Write the sentences again. Use *not*.

Remember! doesn't = does not
don't = do not

1 Lulu plays football.   Lulu does not play football.

2 Molly walks to school.   _____

3 Joe gets up at six o'clock.   _____

4 The boys wear trainers to school. _____

1 Write the missing numbers.

10 _____   30 _____   50 _____

_____ twenty   _____ forty   _____ sixty   _____

2 🎧 Listen and write the numbers.

A Look and write.

1 In Picture 1 how many apples are there? _____

2 In Picture 2 how many toys are there? _____

3 In picture 3 how many children are there? _____

4 In Picture 4 how many cakes are there? _____

70 _____   90 _____

eighty _____   a hundred

2

3 Ask and answer.

In picture 1 how many red apples are there?

There are fifty.

Picture 1 – green apples?
Picture 2 – planes?
Picture 2 – dolls?
Picture 3 – boys?
Picture 3 – girls?
Picture 4 – pink cakes?
Picture 4 – chocolate cakes?

4 Who is saying this?

1   Don't touch it!

2   Eat it!

3   Don't sing loudly.

4   Please, buy them!

4 [image of grandmother and boy with cakes]

B Complete the commands. Use the words in the box. | wear   go   touch   make |

1 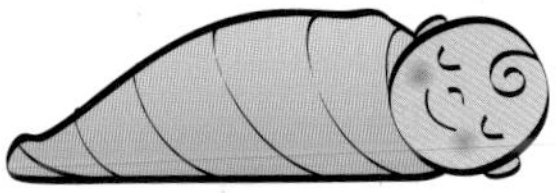   The baby is sleeping. _Don't make_ a noise!

2   Those spines are sharp. _____ them!

3 [image of shark fin]   Look! A shark! _____ in the water!

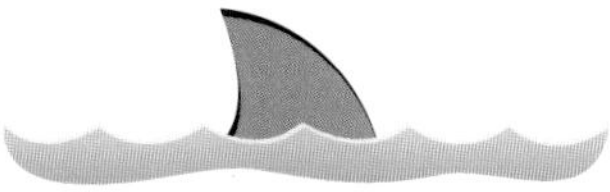

4    It isn't sunny. _____ them!

1 **Name the clothes.**

1   2   3   4   5   6   7   8   9

2 **Talk about the picture.**

A **Complete the sentences.**

1 Lulu is wearing a pink __skirt__ and a blue __hat__ .

2 Alfie is wearing an orange _____ and red _____ .

3 Molly has got blue _____ and red _____ .

4 Miss Carey has got a purple _____ and grey _____ .

10 11 12 13 14

3 Ask and answer.

Whose hat is this?

It's Lulu's.

Whose trousers are these?

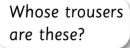

They're Max's.

1 2

3 4

5 6

7 8

B Write.

Remember! It's = It is   They're = They are

1  Whose jumper is this? _____It is Molly's._____

2 Whose trainers are these? _____

3  Whose skirt is this?_____

4  Whose trousers are these? _____

1 🎧 Look and listen.

A Complete the sentences with *was* or *were*.

1 It _____ a hot, sunny day.

2 There _____ monkeys in the trees.

3 There _____ three little fish in the rock pool.

4 _____ it a shark? No, it _____ a dolphin.

2 Answer the questions.

Look at the first picture.
Where were the children?
What was the weather like?

Look at the second picture.
What were there in the trees?
What colour were the rocks?

Look at the third picture.
How many fish were there?
What colour was the crab?

Look at the fourth picture.
Who wanted to swim?

Look at the fifth picture.
What was there in the water?

Look at the sixth picture.
Was it a shark?
What was it?

3 Tell the story.

B Complete the sentences. Use the words in the box.

| next to | behind | between | in front of |

1 The house is _____ the trees.

2 The boy is _____ the boat.

3 The girl _____ her father.

4 The elephant is _____ the tree.

1 🎧 **Look and listen.**

1

ZOO PARK

Yesterday we visited the animal park.

2

We watched the monkeys.

4

There were crocodiles in the river.

A Correct the sentences.

1 Molly liked the snakes. ___No, Molly liked the giraffes.___

2 The lions played in the trees. _____

3 The hippo opened its tiny mouth. _____

4 Lulu liked the parrots. _____

2 Correct the sentences.

3

I liked the giraffes.

Lulu liked the snakes.

No, Lulu liked the crocodiles.

1 The children visited the aquarium.
2 Miss Carey liked the lions.
3 The hippo opened its eyes.
4 The parrots climbed the trees.
5 The monkeys were not funny.
6 Molly liked the eagles.

5

There was a hippo in the river, too.

B Complete the sentences. Use the words in the box.

Use the past tense.   watch   play   climb   visit

1 Yesterday the children _____ the animal park.

2 Alfie _____ a tree in the park.

3 Molly and Lulu _____ TV after school.

4 Max _____ basketball in the playground.

Reading

The first day in school

Lesson	Time	Monday	Tu
1	8.15	Maths	En
2	9.00	Science	Sp
3	9.45	English	Ar
	10.30	Break	B
4	11.00	Sports	Sc
5	11.45	Art	Mu
6	12.30	Music	Ma

Alfie, Molly, Max and Lulu were in school today. They were in a new class. Their teacher was Miss Carey. There was a timetable on the wall. The lessons were on the timetable.

$$700 + 35 = 735$$

$$20 \times 30 = 600$$

The first lesson was at quarter past eight. It was Maths. There were lots of big numbers but the sums were easy.

The second lesson was Science. There was a pretty plant in a jar. It was very interesting.

The third lesson was at quarter to ten. It was English. It was difficult. There were lots of new words on the board. The children learned them.

At half past ten it was break. Alfie, Molly, Max and Lulu were in the playground. Their friends were in the playground, too. It was fun.

The fourth lesson was at eleven o'clock. It was Sports. The children played basketball.It was exciting.

At quarter to twelve the lesson was Art. There were paints and brushes. The children painted dolphins. It was very quiet in the art lesson.

At half past twelve the lesson was Music. The children were in the music room. There was a piano and there were three drums and two guitars. It was not a quiet lesson!

Reading comprehension and vocabulary

1 Circle the right answer.

1 Alfie, Molly, Max and Lulu were in a new   class   school

2 Miss Carey was their new   timetable   teacher

3 At quarter past eight the lesson was   Maths   Science

4 The sums were   difficult   easy

5 The Science lesson was   exciting   interesting

6 The Art lesson was   quick   quiet

7 The Music lesson was in the   music room   classroom

2 Find the pictures for the lessons. Write the numbers.

English ___5___ _____   Sports _____ _____   Art _____ _____

Music _____ _____   Science _____ _____   Maths _____ _____

1    2    3    4

5    6 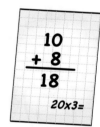   7    8

9    10    11    12

3 Write the picture number.

a plant _____   b sums _____   c guitar _____   d jar _____

Speaking

1 Talk about the picture. 🎧 Then listen.　　**2** 🎧 Listen and read.

Save Henry!
Part 1: That's interesting!

 Look at this picture, children. What is it?

 It's a farm.

 Yes, that's right. And today we're going to a farm.

 Really?

 Yes! We can do Maths and Science and English at the farm.

 Wow! That's exciting.

 What's the name of the farm, Miss Carey?

 Its name is Pear Tree Farm.

 Are there animals on the farm, Miss Carey?

 Yes, there are lots of animals there.

 Where is the farm, Miss Carey?

 It's here. In the city.

 A farm in the city?

 That's interesting!

 Do you want to visit it?

 Yes, please, Miss Carey!

3 🎧 Listen and say.　　**4** Talk about the story.　　**5** Now you!

Grammar

1 Look!

It was sunny yesterday.

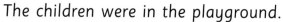

The children were in the playground.

Correct the sentences.

1 Yesterday the children were at the beach.
2 Their grandmother was with them.
3 The weather was cold and wet.
4 The sky was grey and the clouds were black.
5 The moon was high in the sky.
6 Two cats were on the wall.

2 Look!

Was the weather cold yesterday?

No, it wasn't.

Were the children at school?

Yes, they were.

Ask and answer.

1 the weather – hot?
3 Grandma – with them?
5 the clouds - white?

2 the children – at the beach?
4 the sky – grey?
6 the children – happy?

Grammar in conversation

1 🎧 **Listen and read.**

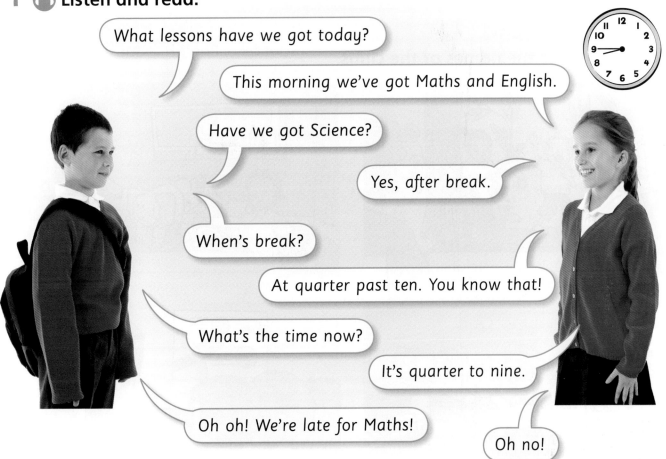

What lessons have we got today?

This morning we've got Maths and English.

Have we got Science?

Yes, after break.

When's break?

At quarter past ten. You know that!

What's the time now?

It's quarter to nine.

Oh oh! We're late for Maths!

Oh no!

2 🎧 **Listen and say.**

3 **Now you!**

4 🎧 **Listen and sing.**

What's the time?
Half past eight.
Oh, no! I'm late, I'm late!

Where's my book?
Where's my pen?
Oh, no! I'm late again.

Run, run, run,
Through the gate,
Never early, always late!

Listening

After-school clubs are great!

1 Look and write the names of the clubs.

Science English Music Art

_____ club

_____ club

_____ club

_____ club

2 🎧 **Listen and number the pictures.**

Phonics 🎧

Look and listen!

ar   jar

There's a plant in a jar.

There's a boy in a car

There's a star in the dark.

and a shark in the park.

→ Now look at WB p7 Use of English

Class composition

1 Read.

Time	Tuesday
9.00	Sports
9.45	Science
10.30	Maths

On Tuesday morning Alfie, Molly, Max and Lulu were in school again. The timetable was on the wall.

2 Look at the pictures. Write about the lessons. Choose words from the box.

easy	interesting	noisy
difficult	exciting	fun

At nine o'clock the lesson was _____ . The children _____ . It was _____

_____

_____

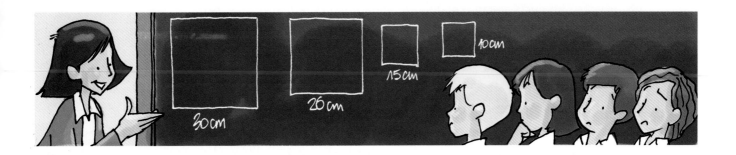

_____

_____

On the farm

Reading 🔊 ## Jack and the beanstalk

Jack lived on a small farm with his mother. They were very poor. One day Jack's mother said, "My dear son, please take our cow to the town. Sell her. Come back with the money."

Jack walked across the fields to the river. A man was on the bridge.
"That's a beautiful cow," he said. "I've got five special beans. Please give your cow to me and take these beans."

He showed the beans to Jack. "They're very pretty colours," said Jack. "Please take my cow and give your beans to me." Jack smiled. He was pleased with the special beans.

Jack walked home. He showed the beans to his mother but she was cross. She pushed them out of Jack's hand. All the special beans were on the ground. "Go to bed, Jack," she said.

In the morning, Jack looked out of the window.
A huge beanstalk was next to the house.
The top of the beanstalk was above the clouds.
Jack climbed the beanstalk.

At the top was a huge castle. Jack counted six tall, gold towers. He opened the large door and walked quietly inside.

An ugly giant lived in the castle. He was asleep in the huge kitchen. Next to the enormous giant was a tiny brown hen in a small gold cage. The hen looked sadly at Jack.

"Please, help me," it said. "I always live in this cage. I cannot walk. I cannot open my wings. I never see the sky."

Jack opened the cage and picked up the little hen. He walked quickly to the beanstalk and he climbed down.

Just then the giant opened his eyes. "Where is my hen?" he shouted. The angry giant walked to the beanstalk and he looked down. "I can see you!" he roared at Jack. "I am coming!"

Jack jumped onto the ground.
He picked up an axe and chopped down the beanstalk.

The giant did not climb down the beanstalk.

The little hen clucked happily. A shiny gold egg was on the ground. Jack and his mother were surprised. It was a very special hen!

Reading comprehension and vocabulary

1 Who said it? Read the sentences. Circle the person.

1 Come back with the money.	the man	Jack's mother
2 I've got five special beans.	Jack	the man
3 They're very pretty colours.	the man	Jack
4 Go to bed.	Jack's mother	Jack
5 I cannot walk.	the giant	the hen
6 Where is my hen?	Jack	the giant
7 I can see you!	the giant	Jack's mother

2 Write the words under the correct picture.

| ugly | poor | little | surprised | brown | special | angry | cross | enormous |

_____   _____   _____

_____   _____   _____

_____   _____   _____

3 Read these words.

| cross | tiny | asleep | small | pretty | huge | large | angry |

Find two words for *little*. Write them here. _____ _____

Find two words for *enormous*. Write them here. _____ _____

Speaking

1 Talk about the picture. 🎧 Then listen.   **2 🎧 Listen and read.**

 Good morning, Mr Oats.

 Good morning, Miss Carey. Welcome to Pear Tree Farm.

 Thank you!

 What animals have you got on the farm, Mr Oats?

 I've got cows, sheep and goats.

 I can see hens.

 I can see a horse.

 That's Henry. He's a beautiful horse.

He's fantastic.

 Mr Oats, what happened to your farm? Look at the house! The windows are broken.

 We had a terrible storm last night - thunder and lightning, wind and rain. Look at my new tractor!

 Oh dear!

 Look at Henry's stable! There are holes in the roof.

 Look at the barn! It hasn't got a roof.

 And there's water everywhere.

 Don't climb on the gate, Alfie!

 Oops! Sorry, Mr Oats!

 Crack!

3 🎧 Listen and say.   **4 Talk about the story.**   **5 Now you!**

Grammar

1 Look!

Lulu looked at the horse.

Hello, goats!

Talk about the picture. Use the words in the boxes.

talked	climbed	liked		farmer	sheep	gate
watched	lived	helped		goats	stable	horse

1 Lulu...   2 The horse...   3 Max...

4 Molly...   5 The dog...   6 Alfie...

2 Look!

Did the horse live in the barn?

Did the cows live in the barn?

No, it didn't.

Yes, they did.

Ask and answer.

1 Molly – help – farmer ?   4 Alfie – climb – gate ?

2 Lulu – like – horse ?   5 dog – watch – hens ?

3 cows – live – stable ?   6 Max – talk – goats ?

Grammar in conversation

1 🎧 **Listen and read.**

What did you do at the weekend?

I visited my friend.

Did you have a good time?

Yes, I did.

What did you do?

We played football.

Did you watch TV?

No, we didn't.
We played computer games.

It sounds great.

Yes, it was fun.

2 🎧 **Listen and say.**

3 **Now you! These words can help you:** | play   watch   climb   jump   walk

4 🎧 **Listen and sing.**

The weekend, the weekend, we love the weekend!
Time to sleep and time to play,
Time for laughter all the day.
Time for friends and family,
Time for funny films on TV.
Time to read and time to run,
Time for games and time for fun.
Time for quiet, time for noise.
It's the weekend, girls and boys!
The weekend, the weekend, we love the weekend!
The weekend, the weekend, we love the weekend!

Listening

John and Sue visited their grandparents.

1 🎧 **Listen.**

2 Circle the right answers.

1 Grandma and Grandpa have   A a shop.   B a farm.   C a castle.

2 Grandma and Grandpa have lots of   A horses   B dogs   C animals.

3 Did John and Sue have fun?   A Yes, they did.   B No, they didn't.

3 🎧 **What animals were there? Listen again and ✓.**

Phonics 🎧   Look and listen!

ou   mouse

The round moon is shining above the house.
The clouds are silver and white. Look there,
on the ground. It's a little grey mouse.
Hush! Don't make a sound!

→ Now look at WB p17 Use of English

Class composition

1 **Read. Finish the story. Use the words in the box.**

| walk | jump up | push | ugly | scared | under |

Once upon a time three hungry goats were in a field.
They looked at the tall green plants across the river.

The first goat _____
on the bridge. An _____ man
was _____ the bridge.

The man _____
The first goat was _____
He _____ not _____ over the bridge.

The second _____

_____

_____

_____

_____

_____

_____

_____

_____

_____

_____

_____

_____

_____

Reading 🎧

A helicopter pilot

helicopter
This can fly at 200 kilometres an hour.

helmet

headset

sunglasses

earphones
The pilot listens to
people on the ground.

microphone
The pilot can speak to
people on the ground.

This pilot flies a helicopter. The helicopter can fly quickly over mountains. It can land on hills. It is smaller than a plane but it is faster than a motorbike. The pilot's job is often exciting.

The pilot wears a helmet. It is very hard. The helmet protects his head. He wears sunglasses. Sometimes the sun shines very brightly. The sunglasses protect his eyes.
The pilot wears a headset under his helmet. Sometimes he talks to a lifeguard on a beach. Sometimes he talks to a fireman at a fire. He speaks into the microphone. He can hear people through the earphones.

A hospital nurse

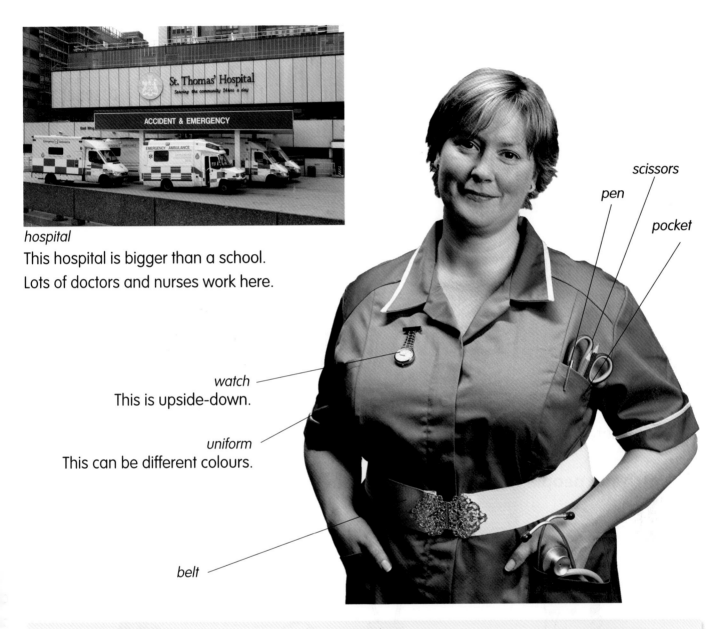

hospital
This hospital is bigger than a school.
Lots of doctors and nurses work here.

scissors

pen

pocket

watch
This is upside-down.

uniform
This can be different colours.

belt

This nurse works in a hospital. There are lots of people in the hospital and she is always busy. Sometimes people come to the hospital by helicopter. The nurse's job is interesting but sometimes it is difficult, too.

She wears a blue uniform. She wears a white belt. She has a watch on her uniform. She can always look at the time easily and quickly.

She carries a pen in her pocket. She writes notes about the people in the hospital. She carries scissors too. These are useful in her job.

Reading comprehension and vocabulary

1 Read. Write *true* or *false*. Correct the false sentences.

1 A helicopter can fly at 200 kph. _____

2 A helicopter is smaller than a motorbike. _____

3 The helmet protects the pilot's hands. _____

4 The hospital is bigger than a school. _____

5 The nurse is never busy. _____

6 She wears a blue watch. _____

2 Match. Write the letter.

a   b   c   d   e

headset ____   helmet ____   watch ____   pocket ____   belt ____

3 Match the people and the jobs. Write the letter.

1 fireman ☐   2 doctor ☐   3 lifeguard ☐

a   b   c

Read and write the number.

A He helps people on the beach. He watches people in the sea. ____

B He helps people when there is a fire. He wears a helmet. ____

C He helps people in a hospital. He works with the nurses. ____

Speaking

1 Talk about the picture. ⬤ **Then listen.**   **2** ⬤ **Listen and read.**

Save Henry!
Part 3: Here come the workmen!

 Here come the workmen!

 The builder can mend the barn and the house.

 The painter can paint the house.

 The plumber can fix the water pipes.

 The carpenter can mend the stable and the gate!

 Alfie, you can help him.

 OK!

 Take your ruler. How wide is the gate? How high is it?

 I've got my camera. I can take photos.

 Excellent!

 Max and I can write about everything. Come on, Max!

 Oh dear, oh dear!

 What's the matter, Mr Oats?

 How can I pay these workmen? I'm not a rich man.

Oh dear, oh dear! There's only one thing I can do.

 What's that?

 I can sell Henry.

 Henry? Your beautiful horse? Oh no!

 Hello? Channel 10?

3 ⬤ **Listen and say.**   **4 Talk about the picture.**   **5 Now you!**

Grammar

1 Look!

> The helicopter is fast.

> The plane is faster.

Point and say.

1 big

2 tall

3 soft

4 loud

5 small

6 slow

2 Look!

> Which is taller? The giraffe or the elephant?

> The giraffe is taller than the elephant.

Ask and answer.

1 faster

2 older

3 bigger

4 smaller

5 longer

6 hotter

Unit 3 Comparative adjectives: *fast, faster (than)*

Grammar in conversation

1 🎧 **Listen and read.**

How tall are you, Ben?

I'm 1 metre 50 centimetres.

I'm 1 metre 40 centimetres.

I'm taller than you.

How long is your hand?

I don't know.

Let's measure it.

It's 12 centimetres long.

How wide is your hand?

It's 8 centimetres wide.

Your hand is wider than my hand.

It's longer, too.

2 🎧 **Listen and say.**

3 **Now you!**

4 🎧 **Listen and say.**

I'm higher than the tree tops.
I'm bigger than a house.
I'm stronger than a lion.
I'm quieter than a mouse.

I'm brighter than a candle.
I'm wider than the sea.
I'm older than the silver moon.
Do you know my name? Tell me!

Listening

1 🔊 **Look, listen and point.**

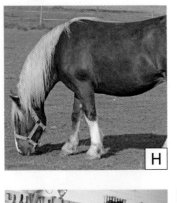 H

 T

 L

 A

 E

 P

 E

 N

2 🔊 **Look, listen and write the letters.**

1	2	3	4	5	6	7	8
☐	☐	☐	☐	☐	☐	☐	☐

What's the word?

Phonics 🔊

Look and listen!

ay   play

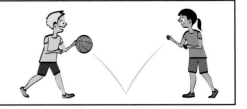

It's Monday today.

My birthday's in May.

Please stay and play.

Let's all say Hooray!

➡ Now look at WB p27 Use of English

Class composition

1 **Look and write. The verbs in the box can help you.**

A lifeguard

work

help

swim

wear

protect

speak

watch

hat

sunglasses

T-shirt

phone

shorts

sandals

The lifeguard can _____
in the sea in these shorts.

_____

_____

_____

_____

_____

_____

_____

Revision 1

I am mending the barn.

I am mending the wall.

How tall is the gate?

It's one metre tall. How wide is it?.

I am fixing the water.

It's two metres wide.

The insects are eating the plant. The hens are eating the insects.

That's right, Max. Write it down please.

HENRY

I am writing about the hen. I am drawing the hen.

Very good, Molly.

I am painting the stable.

1 What animals were in the farmyard? How many animals were there?

2 Which is bigger?  Which is smaller?

3 Which is louder? 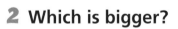 Which is faster?

4 What are they? What did they do?

5 What subjects did they do?

Project 1

Draw or make a farmyard. Draw or make the buildings and animals.

1 Write about the buildings. Answer these questions:

How tall is it? How wide is it? How long is it? Who mended or fixed it?

2 Find out about animals. Look on the internet or in a book.

Write about the animals. Answer these questions: How tall is it? Where does it live? What does it eat?

3 Talk about the things in the farmyard.

The goats live in the field.

The stable is 3 metres tall.

The plumber fixed the water.

The sheep is 1 metre tall.

The horse is in the stable. It is bigger than the sheep.

Things we use

The American pioneers

A hundred years ago many people travelled across America. They needed houses and fields. They were pioneers. A pioneer does something first. These people travelled across America first.

They stopped near a river. They needed wood and water. They used axes and they chopped down trees. The horses pulled the logs with ropes. The men lifted one log on top of another log. These were the walls of their house.

Inside there were two rooms. In one room there was a fire. The women cooked food in big pots. The children helped. They picked up wood for the fire. They fetched water from the river.

There were not many toys. The girls skipped with a rope. The boys played skittles. All the children played a game with a cup and a ball. You can make this game, too.

Cup and ball game

You need:

A4 paper

colours

10 cm sticky tape

30 cm string or wool

1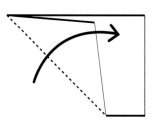
Fold the paper.

2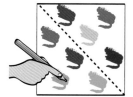
Cut. Keep the small piece of paper.

3
Open out the big piece. Turn it over. Colour it.

4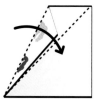
Turn over the paper again. Fold it.

5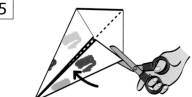
Fold it again and cut.

6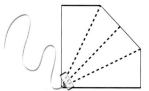
Open the paper. Stick the string onto it.

7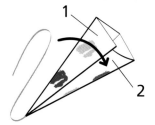
Put side 1 on top of side 2.

8
Stick it.

9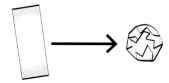
Make the small piece of paper into a ball.

10
Stick it on the end of the string.

11
Swing the ball up into the air.

12
Catch it in the cup.

Reading comprehension and vocabulary

1 Choose the correct word.

1 The pioneers needed _____ and fields. (horses / houses)

2 They _____ near a river. (stopped / skipped)

3 The pioneers used _____ and they chopped down trees. (scissors / axes)

4 The _____ pulled the logs with ropes. (horses / men)

5 The women cooked _____ in big pots. (fire / food)

6 The children fetched _____ from the river. (water / wood)

7 The children played a game with a cup and a _____. (ball / bag)

2 Write the word.

axe	wool	scissors	wood	string	rope

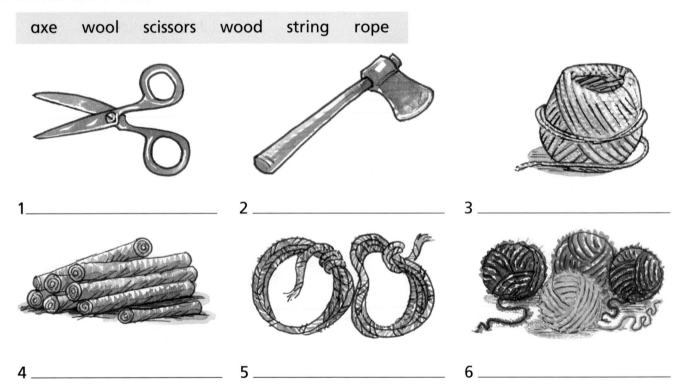

1_____ 2_____ 3_____

4_____ 5_____ 6_____

3 Complete the sentences .

1 The pioneers travelled across _____.

2 There were _____ rooms in the house.

3 In one room there was a _____.

4 There were not many _____.

Speaking

1 Talk about the picture. 🎧 Then listen.   **2** 🎧 Listen and read.

 Children! We have a visitor this morning.

 Good morning! I'm Gary West. I work for Channel 10.

 The TV channel? Wow!

 Can you tell me about the farm?

 The farm's great but last night there was a terrible storm.

 Look at the tractor!

 Look at the broken windows and the roofs!

 But there are carpenters here with saws and hammers and nails.

 The builder is fixing a new metal gate.

 The plumber is fixing new plastic pipes.

 But Mr Oats, the farmer, is a very poor man.

 Hmm... Do you know about 'My TV'?

 Yes, it's a competition for children.

 That's right. The winners make a TV programme.

 Just a minute! I've got a great idea!

 What's that, Max?

 We can enter the competition!

 Perhaps we can make a TV programme!

 We can tell people about Pear Tree Farm!

 Perhaps we can save Henry!

3 🎧 Listen and say.   **4** Talk about the story.   **5** Now you!

Grammar

1 Look!

What do you remember about pioneers in America?

Did the pioneers travel in cars?

No, they didn't.

Did the women cook over fires?

Yes, they did.

Ask and answer.

1 chop down ?

2 use ?

3 play ?

4 play ?

5 cook ?

6 need ?

2 Look!

The children cooked the food.

No! The women cooked the food.

Correct the sentences.

1 The women chopped down trees.

2 The children pulled the logs.

3 The horses fetched water.

4 The boys skipped with a rope.

5 The girls played skittles.

6 The men picked up wood for the fire.

Grammar in conversation

1 🎧 Listen and read.

fetched	used	watched	river	pot	children
needed	played	cooked	skittles	rope	horse

Let's play a word game.

OK. How do you play it?

You choose two words and make a sentence.

Right. You start.

OK. Your words are 'fetched' and 'river'.

That's easy!
The boys fetched water from the river.

Very good. You get one point.

Now it's your turn. Your words are 'cooked' and 'skittles'.

Oh! That's hard! Umm...umm...

Yes.

Do you give up?

Ha ha! You get no points at all!

2 🎧 Listen and say.

3 Now you!

4 🎧 Listen and say.

I like coffee, I like tea,
I want Sally here with me.
One, two, three, four,
Out you go and shut the door!

Listening

1 🎧 **Look, listen and point.**

2 🎧 **Listen again and write the letters.**   1 _____   2 _____   3 _____   4 _____

3 🎧 **Listen to the questions and circle the right answers.**

1 one   two

2 from the river   from the pond

3 in the afternoon   in the evening

4 Yes, she did.   No, she didn't.

Phonics 🎧

Look and listen!

ow   snow

Blow, wind, blow.
Blow the white snow.
Throw the white snow
At our yellow window.

➡ Now look at WB p37 Use of English

Class composition

1 Read about the game of skittles.

Pioneer children played skittles.
They used a ball and nine tall pieces of wood.
They rolled the ball at the skittles.

You can make a small game of skittles. You can use paper.
This is what you do:
You draw nine squares. You cut the squares. You keep the small piece of paper.
You colour the squares. You roll them then you stick them. You make nine skittles.
You squash the small piece of paper into a ball. Now you can play the game.

2 Look at the pictures. Complete the instructions.

You need:

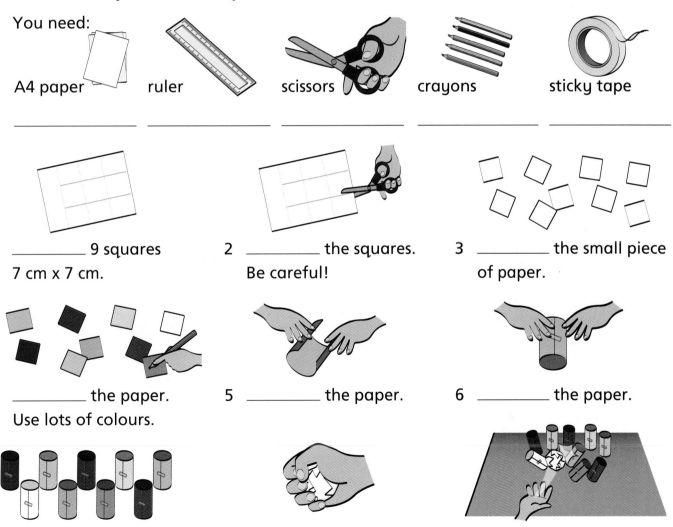

A4 paper   ruler   scissors   crayons   sticky tape

_____   _____   _____

1 _____ 9 squares
7 cm x 7 cm.

2 _____ the squares.
Be careful!

3 _____ the small piece
of paper.

4 _____ the paper.
Use lots of colours.

5 _____ the paper.

6 _____ the paper.

7 _____ 9 skittles.

8 _____ the white
paper into a ball.

9 _____ the game.

Let's listen to music!

Do you like music? Do you listen at home? Look at the pictures on these pages. These machines play music. There are old machines and new machines.

cylinder

First there was the phonograph. Thomas Edison invented it in 1877. He recorded music onto the cylinder. The cylinder is wood and metal. It turned round and round. It played the music.

disc

After that there was the gramophone. It played round, flat discs. There were songs on the discs. Usually, there was only one singer and a piano.

Many people liked these big gramophones. A family listened together in their living room.

Next, people invented the microphone. They recorded big bands. There were lots of drums, trumpets and singers. It was very exciting. Lots of people wanted the music.

microphone

The new gramophones were smaller. They were plastic and wood. The plastic was bright and colourful. The discs were plastic, too, and they were big.

CD

Later, people invented a smaller plastic disc. It was the CD. You can play a CD on a small machine. This is a CD player. You can easily use this in your bedroom.

This is a very small machine. It's an iPod*. People can listen to music in the street or on the bus. They use earphones.

earphones

This boy is listening to a very big band and the music player is in his hands!

Reading comprehension and vocabulary

1 Put the sentences in order. Write the number.

a It played round, flat discs. _____

b Later people invented a smaller plastic disc. _____

c Next people invented the microphone. _____

d First there was the phonograph. _____

e You can play a CD on a small machine. _____

f They recorded big bands. _____

g After that there was the gramophone. _____

h It was the CD. _____

2 Match. Write the letter.

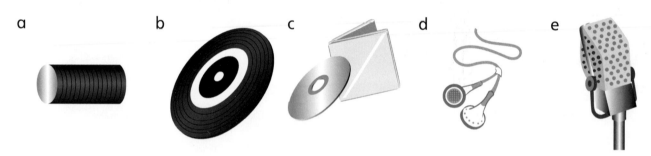

a   b   c   d   e

1 CD _____   2 microphone _____   3 cylinder _____   4 earphones _____   5 disc _____

3 Complete the sentences. Use the past tense.

| like | turn | invent | listen | record | play |

1 Thomas Edison _____*invented*_____ the phonograph in 1877.

2 He _____ music onto the cylinder.

3 The cylinder _____ round and round.

4 The gramophone _____ round, flat discs.

5 Lots of people _____ these big gramophones.

6 A family _____ together in their living room.

Speaking

1 Talk about the picture.  Then listen.　　**2**  Listen and read.

Save Henry!
Part 5: The competition

 OK. Let's talk about the competition.

 We need good ideas.

 I can take photos with my camera.

 I can take photos with my mobile phone.

 My dad's got a video camera. We can use that.

 Fantastic! We can video the farm.

 We can interview Mr Oats.

 Good idea, Lulu!

 We can interview the animals!

 Don't be silly, Molly!

 It's not a bad idea, you know.

 We can do their voices.

 Yes! That's funny!

 We need music. We need a song about Henry.

 Or a rap! Listen to this!

Pear Tree Farm is a really cool place.

Henry the horse can put a smile on your face.

 We can call the programme 'Save Henry!'

 I like it!

3  Listen and say.　　**4** Talk about the story.　　**5** Now you!

Grammar

1 Look!

Molly's dad has got a shop.

There was a woman outside the shop.

Molly was in the shop yesterday.

There were guitars in the window.

Read and say *Yes* or *No*.

1 There were CDs in the window.
3 There were trumpets in the window.
5 There was a woman in the shop.

2 There were two boys in the shop.
4 There was a camera in the window.
6 There was one drum in the window.

2 Look!

Was there a boy in the shop?

Yes, there was.

No, there wasn't.

Were there trumpets in the window?

Yes, there were.

No, there weren't.

Ask and answer.

1  window? 2 window? 3 shop?

4 shop? 5 window? 6 shop?

Grammar in conversation

1 🎧 **Listen and read.**

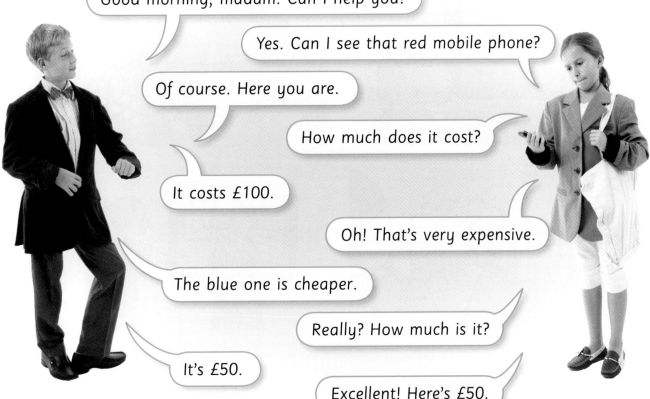

Good morning, madam. Can I help you?

Yes. Can I see that red mobile phone?

Of course. Here you are.

How much does it cost?

It costs £100.

Oh! That's very expensive.

The blue one is cheaper.

Really? How much is it?

It's £50.

Excellent! Here's £50.

2 🎧 **Listen and say.**

3 Now you!

4 🎧 **Listen and sing.**

Brring, brring! Hello, hello!
Brring, brring! Hello, hello!
Who's that? Is that you?
　Yes, it's me. Who are you?
Me! Me! How are you?
　Fine! Fine! But who are you?
Speak up! I can't hear you.
　You can't hear who?
You! You!

What are you doing?
　What am I doing?
Yes, what are you doing?
　I'm talking to you!
Brring, brring! Hello! Hello!
Brring, brring! Hello! Hello!
Brring, brring! Brring, brring! ...

Listening

1 Look!

2 Listen and write the letters.

1 _____   2 _____   3 _____   4 _____

3 Listen again and answer the questions.

1 What do the children say?
2 Has the video camera got a microphone?
3 Where is the boy's iPod?
4 What is the film like?

Phonics

Look and listen!

ir   first

First the girl has got a bird
and wears a bright yellow skirt.
Then the girl has got her bird
and wears a blue T-shirt.

➔ Now look at WB p47 Use of English

Unit 5 Listening: matching pictures and dialogues; listening for gist and detail
Phonics: *ir* vowel sound

Class composition

Talk about the pictures and write.

Let's watch TV!

People invented television eighty years ago.

_____?

_____?

screen

First there was

_____

_____

_____

_____

_____

_____

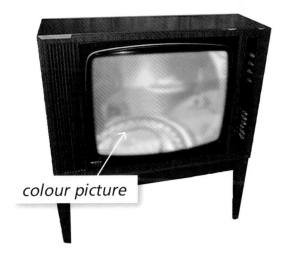

colour picture

flat screen

good picture

Reading

The International Games are fantastic!

The Bridge Hotel

116 River Street

South City

24th July

Dear Grandma,

I hope you are well. We are all fine. Are you having good weather? The weather is very good here. It is getting hotter and hotter! I am having a great time. The International Games are fantastic. Mum and Dad are having a great time, too.

On Monday morning we went to the gymnastics competition. There was a very young man in the competition. He was only sixteen and he came from Russia. He was very strong . We all sat quietly and watched him. He was amazing. At the end, we all jumped up and clapped loudly. He won a silver medal and he smiled happily.

On Monday afternoon we watched the men's judo competition. People wear big white trousers and jackets for judo. They leave their shoes next to a big square mat then they step onto it. They hold onto each other. They push and pull and turn. One person falls down and the other person wins a point. It is an old sport and it is very interesting.

On Tuesday we went to the sailing competition. We saw boats from all over the world. It was windy and the boats sailed really fast. The huge sails were beautiful bright colours. A boat with a blue and green sail won the gold medal.

Yesterday morning we watched the cycling competition. The men went round and round the track faster and faster. It was very exciting. In the afternoon we watched the show jumping. The horses jumped over big gates and over water. They went really fast, too.

Do you remember? Dad likes skiing. The skiing competition is in December. People travel to the mountains. There is lots of snow. They ski down the mountains. Mum and Dad went last year. They liked it a lot.

I am sending you some photos of the sports. They are Dad's pictures. They are really great.

Lots of love from

Peter

Reading comprehension and vocabulary

1 Answer the questions.

1 Who is Peter writing to?
2 What is the weather like at the International Games?
3 Where did Peter go on Monday morning?
4 What did the young man win?
5 What do people wear for judo?
6 What was the weather like on Tuesday?
7 What did the horses jump over?
8 When is the skiing competition?
9 Where do people travel to?
10 Whose are the pictures?

2 Match. Write the words.

| gymnastics | sailing | judo | show jumping | skiing | cycling |

a _____

b _____

c _____

d _____

e _____

f _____

3 Circle the odd one out.

1 judo   camera   gymnastics   swimming   tennis

2 gold medal   prize   track   cup   silver medal

3 fantastic   exciting   interesting   amazing   windy

Speaking

1 Talk about the picture. Then listen. **2** Listen and read.

Save Henry!
Part 6: At the TV studios

 Hello! Welcome to this year's 'My TV' competition!

 I can't believe it! We're at Channel 10.

 In my hand I've got a golden envelope.

 What's in the envelope?

 In the envelope is the prize money - a lot of money!

 Did you hear that? A lot of money!

 Also in the envelope is the name of this year's winner.

 Who is it? Who's the winner?

 I am very happy to tell you that the winner is...

 Come on! Come on!

 'Save Henry!' Children, please come and get your prize!

 Oh, wow!

 Lulu, Alfie, Molly and Max, congratulations! Please, take the 'My TV' cup and your medals.

 Thank you! Thank you very much!

 Here's your prize money. And good luck with your TV programme!

 Thank you! We believe our programme can help Pear Tree Farm.

 And the prize money can save Henry!

Hooray!

3 Listen and say.   **4** Talk about the story.   **5** Now you!

Grammar

1 Look!

The children went to school.

No, they went to the TV studios.

Read and correct the sentences.

1 The children went to Channel 5.
2 They saw Gary Oats.
3 Lulu sat between Alfie and Max.
4 The children won second prize.
5 Henry said "Congratulations!"
6 The children came home with a tiny cup.

2 Look!

Did the children win third prize?

Did they win first prize?

No, they didn't.

Yes, they did.

Ask and answer. Use the verbs provided.

1 go ?   2 see ?

3 win ?   4 sit next to ?

5 say "Congratulations!" ?   6 come home ?

Grammar in conversation

1  **Listen and read.**

What are you hobbies, Joe?

Well, I like sports. I like playing basketball.

Do you like swimming?

Yes, I love it. How about you?

I don't like sports.

Really?

I like reading and listening to music.

Me, too. Who's your favourite singer?

Suki-Sue.

I like her, too. I've got all her CDs.

She's brilliant!

2 **Listen and say.**

3 **Now you!**

4 **Listen and sing.**

We like running. We like jumping.
How about you? How about you?
Basketball and tennis,
Volleyball and judo,
We like swimming, too,
We like swimming, too.

Listening

1 Name the sports.

skiing sailing judo show jumping

A

B

C

D

2  Listen and write the letters.

1 _____ 2 _____ 3 _____ 4 _____

3 Listen again and answer the questions.

1 Picture B: What is the weather like?
2 Picture D: Is the English man winning?
3 Picture A: What is the name of the horse?
4 Picture C: Is the weather hot or cold?

Phonics Look and listen!

er **painter**

First came the builder,
Then came the carpenter,
Next came the plumber,
And last came the painter.

Look! It's our new house!

➜ Now look at WB p57 Use of English

Class composition

Peter stayed at the International Games. He watched sports on Saturday. Look at the pictures. Write Peter's next letter to his grandma.

_____

_____

_____

_____

Dear _____

 These games are brilliant. On Saturday morning we went to _____

_____

_____

_____

_____

_____

_____

_____

_____

_____

Revision 2

Listen and read. Read again. Talk about Pear Tree Farm then act out the story.

Hello! Welcome to 'My TV'.

Our programme is about Pear Tree Farm. and Mr Oats, the farmer.

Mr Oats loves his farm but it is very old. Is that right, Mr Oats?

Yes. I need a new barn. The gates are falling down and there is water in the yard.

The carpenters and builders came to the farm. They fetched new wood and metal.

They lifted the wood onto the barn.

They used saws, hammers and nails.

They mended the barn, the stable and the gates.

The plumber fixed the water. He used plastic.

The painter painted all the doors.

How much does this work cost, Mr Oats?

It costs a lot!

How can I pay the builders? I can sell Henry.

That's terrible! Poor Henry!

But Mr Oats did not sell Henry. We entered the 'My TV' competition.

And we won!

The prize money saved Henry. Now he can stay at Pear Tree Farm.

We are all very happy! Goodbye! Goodbye!

Project 2

1 Write the story of Mr Oats and Pear Tree Farm.

Think about these questions.

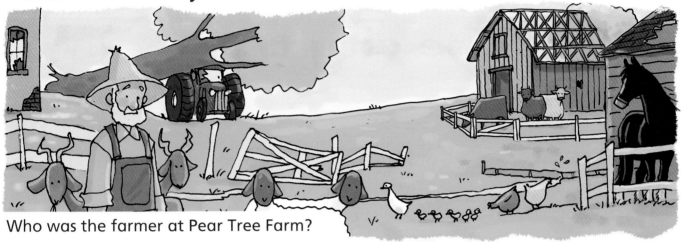

Who was the farmer at Pear Tree Farm?

What animals were at the farm?

What was wrong at Pear Tree Farm?

Who visited the farm?

What men came to the farm?

What did they do?

What did the work cost?

What animal did Mr Oats talk about?

2 Draw pictures. Read your story.

What competition did the children enter?

Did they win?

Did Mr Oats sell Henry?

Who was happy at the end?

Reading

The city train

We're rushing through the station,
We've got tickets for the train.
We're visiting the city
Then we're coming home again.

The train is at the platform
And it's ready to go
We must hurry, hurry, hurry
I can hear the whistle blow.

The red and silver engine,
Is noisy, big and strong
And faster, faster, faster
It is pulling us along.

Now trees and fields are flying by,
Flying by the train.
We're visiting the city
Then we're coming home again.

Welcome home!

Welcome home!
Did you have a good day?
Did you climb the tall tower
In the city today?

> We went to the tower
> And we climbed to the top,
> Then we had a great time
> In the city toy shop.

Did you see the trams?
Did you have a ride?
Did you see the castle?
And did you go inside?

> We saw lots of trams
> But we didn't have a ride.
> We saw the king's castle
> And we went inside.

> The city is fantastic
> And we really liked the train.
> Now we've got a question –
> When can we go again?

Reading comprehension and vocabulary

1 **Answer the questions. Write short answers.**

The city train

(verse 1)	1	Where are the children?	*in the station*
	2	What are they visiting?	
(verse 2)	3	Where is the train?	
(verse 3)	4	What colours is the train?	
(verse 4)	5	What things are flying by the train?	

Welcome home!

(verse 2)	6	Where did the children go first?	
	7	Where did they go next?	
(verse 4)	8	What did they see lots of?	
	9	Whose castle did they go inside?	
(verse 5)	10	What word describes the city?	

2 **Write the words under the correct pictures.**

| station | ticket | platform | engine | tram | whistle |

1 _____   2 _____   3 _____   4 _____   5 _____   6 _____

3 **Circle three words for *go quickly*. Use them to complete the sentences.**

| pull | rush | come | visit | run | climb | hurry |

1 I can win the race. I can _____ fast.

2 The train is ready to go. We must _____

3 Lots of people are _____ through the station today.

Speaking

1 Talk about the picture. Then listen.   **2** Listen and read.

Stop, thief!
Part 1: Hello, Toby!

TICKETS

 Where's Toby? Can you see my cousin?

 Is that him? Is he in the first carriage?

 There are lots of passengers.

 There he is! Look! He's waving.

 Has he got a lot of luggage?

 That's strange. He hasn't got a suitcase.

 Hi, Toby!

 Hello, Alfie.

 What's the matter?

 A boy took my suitcase and he ran away with it.

 Oh! That's terrible!

 All my things are inside. My clothes, my money, my mobile...

 What did he look like?

 He was older than us and he had a red hat.

 Is that him?

 Where?

 Next to the kiosk. Now he's walking past the ticket office.

Yes, that's him and that's my suitcase.

Quick! After him! He mustn't get away!

3 Listen and say.   **4** Talk about the story.   **5** Now you!

Grammar

1 Look!

The West family was on a train.

The girls had drinks.

Mum had the tickets.

Find and say.

2 Look!

Did Grandma have a book?

Yes, she did.

Did the boys have drinks?

No, they didn't.

Ask and answer.

1

2

3

4

5

6

Grammar in conversation

1 🎧 **Listen and read.**

Hi! I'm new. Can you tell me the rules?

Well, you must get to school on time. You mustn't be late.

OK. What else must I do?

You must do your homework.

Of course. What else?

You must be polite.

I'm always polite.

You mustn't shout.

I never shout.

And you must wear your uniform.

Really?

Yes. You mustn't wear those jeans to school.

But I love my jeans!

2 🎧 **Listen and say.**

3 Now you!

4 🎧 **Listen and sing.**

DINOSAUR SCHOOL

At dinosaur school, dinosaur school
These are the dinosaur rules.
You must learn to fight
And you mustn't be polite.
You must stamp and shout
And go running in and out.
You must growl and roar
And always slam the door.
These are the dinosaur rules!

Listening

1 🎧 **Look, listen and point.**

2 🎧 **Listen again and write the letters.**

☐ ☐ ☐ ☐ ☐ ☐ ☐

What's the word?

3 Talk about the picture.

Phonics 🎧

Look and listen!

y   sky

Cry, little duckling, cry
See the swans fly by.

Fly, my pretty swan, fly,
Fly up in the sky.

➡ Now look at WB p67 Use of English

Class composition

1 Complete the poem.

Look at the picture. Where are the children? What can they see?
Read. Choose words to complete each line. Think of a title.

_____

We're up on the _____,	tower castle
We're right at the _____.	end top
Far _____ in the street	above below
There's a _____ by the shop.	taxi bus
It's _____ up here,	quiet noisy
We're near to the _____,	sky ground
The _____ and the sun	clowns clouds
And the birds _____ by.	falling flying
We can _____ the blue river,	sea see
The _____ and boats.	bridges beaches
We can see the _____ farm,	old new
The sheep and the _____.	cows goats
Let's stay ten more _____,	minutes mountains
Let's _____ for an hour.	go stay
_____ stay here all day	Let's Look
At the top of the _____!	tower tree

2 🎧 Listen and say.

Reading 🎧 Aunt Jemima's earring

"This new mall is huge!" said Anna.

"Yes," said Aunt Jemima. "It's bigger than the old mall and it's nicer, too. There are four escalators and a lift. It opened yesterday. It's very exciting."

"I need a new computer disc," said Uncle Bob. "Stay with Aunt Jemima, Anna. We mustn't lose you." He went into the computer shop. Anna and Aunt Jemima waited outside.

Anna looked around. There were lots of people. She looked at the floor. Suddenly she saw a small grey ring. She picked up the ring. It was metal but it wasn't shiny. Anna put it in her pocket.

Uncle Bob came back and they went to the clothes shop. Aunt Jemima wanted a new scarf. She put a pretty scarf round her neck. She looked in the mirror.

"Oh no!" she said. "My earring! It's missing. We must go back to the computer shop."

They looked on the floor outside the computer shop. Then Anna heard a sob. Next to her was a small boy.

"Oh, dear. What's the matter?" asked Anna.

"I dropped my new car," said the boy. "I lost a piece and now it doesn't go." He cried and a big tear fell on the floor.

"Did you lose a ring?" Anna asked.

"Yes," said the boy. "I looked on the floor but I didn't find it. I found this but it isn't mine." The boy had a shiny silver ring in his hand.

"That's Aunt Jemima's earring!" Anna put her hand in her pocket and took out the grey metal ring. "Is this yours?" she asked.

The boy fixed the ring into his car. "Yes," he said. "Thank you."

Anna took the earring to Aunt Jemima. She was very happy. "Now let's have a nice cup of tea in the café," she said.

"Just a minute," said Uncle Bob. "My new disc! It's in the clothes shop."

"Oh, no!" said Anna. "Everyone is losing things today!"

Reading comprehension and vocabulary

1 Who said it? Circle the person.

1 It's very exciting.   A Anna   B Aunt Jemima

2 We mustn't lose you.   A Aunt Jemima   B Uncle Bob

3 We must go back to the computer shop.   A Aunt Jemima   B Uncle Bob

4 What's the matter?   A Aunt Jemima   B Anna

5 Did you lose a ring?   A Uncle Bob   B Anna

6 I looked on the floor but I didn't find it.   A the boy   B Anna

7 Thank you.   A Aunt Jemima   B the boy

8 I left it in the clothes shop.   A Uncle Bob   B Aunt Jemima

2 Name the shops.

| music shop | shoe shop | clothes shop | book shop | computer shop | sports shop |

1 _____   2 _____   3 _____

4 _____   5 _____   6 _____

Speaking

1 Talk about the picture. Then listen.   **2** Listen and read.

Stop, thief!
Part 2: At the supermarket

What's he doing in this supermarket?

Perhaps he's hungry.

Where is he? Can you see him?

Is that him behind the vegetables?

Yes, I can see his red hat.

Hey, you! Stop!

There he goes!

He's running past the bread and cakes.

How can we catch him?

We can go left.

And we can go right.

Good idea!

Where is he?

Sshh! He's behind those tins of beans.

CRASH!

Oh! Be careful, Max!

He's running away!

Quick! After him!

Stop, thief!

3 Listen and say.   **4** Talk about the story.   **5** Now you!

Grammar

1 Look!

The children saw the thief.

The thief had Toby's suitcase.

Make sentences. Write the letters.

1 Toby put his clothes	A his clothes, his mobile and his money.
2 The thief took	B the crash.
3 Toby lost	C Toby's suitcase.
4 The children found the thief	D into his suitcase.
5 The tins of beans fell	E in the supermarket.
6 The thief heard	F onto the floor.

1 <u>D</u> 2 ____ 3 ____ 4 ____ 5 ____ 6 ____

2 Look!

Did the children see the thief?

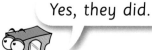

Yes, they did.

Did the thief come back?

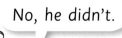

No, he didn't.

Ask and answer.

1 Toby - put - mobile - into - pocket ? 2 thief - take - suitcase ?

3 thief - go - into - clothes shop ? 4 children - see - thief ?

5 thief - run - out of - supermarket ? 6 children - catch - thief ?

Grammar in conversation

1 🎧 **Listen and read.**

What did you do at the weekend?

I went shopping with my mum.

Really? Where did you go?

We went to the new mall.

Oh! What's it like?

It's huge!

What did you buy?

I bought jeans, shoes, a jacket and two CDs.

Wow! Did you spend lots of money?

No, I didn't.
My mum spent lots of money!

2 🎧 **Listen and say.**

3 Now you!

4 🎧 **Listen and say.**

Big shop in the town,
Lifts going up and down,
Doors going round about,
People going in and out.

MEGASTORE

Listening

1 **Look and write the names of the shops.** shoe   music   book   sports

_____ shop

A

_____ shop

B

_____ shop

C

_____ shop

D

2 **Listen and write the letters.**

1 _____   2 _____   3 _____   4 _____

3 **Listen again and answer the questions.**

1 Can the girl have the pink shoes?
3 What book does the boy want?

2 Who wants to buy CDs?
4 Are the boots cheap or expensive?

Phonics   Look and listen!

oa   boat

A boat can float on the water.

A goat in a boat can float on the water.

A goat in a coat in a boat can float on the water

but a goat in a coat in a boat can't float on the road.

→ Now look at WB p77 Use of English

Class composition

Anna found Aunt Jemima's earring. What happened next? Write the story.

hurry back   clothes shop

Anna, Aunt Jemima and Uncle Bob
hurried back to

look for   disc   shelf

find   under   chair

saw   dress   like

carry   bags   café   people

sit   have   tea   cakes

Street shows

How do they do that?

The city streets are busy today. People are walking through the market. There are shops and colourful stalls – and there are street shows!

This woman is a juggler. She is wearing colourful clothes. Sometimes she juggles with balls. Today she is juggling with long, fat sticks. She throws a stick into the air, then another and another and another. She catches each stick. Then she quickly throws it again. The sticks go round in a circle. She is juggling. A small boy is watching her. It's amazing!

This man is a fire blower. He holds a stick. There is a small flame at the end. He blows over the small flame. He must be careful. There is fire! How does he do it?

This man is a stilt walker. He is taller than the walls around the park. He is the tallest person in the park.
His clothes are very long. Does he look funny? He is walking on stilts. The stilts are under his trousers. Stilt walking is not easy. He mustn't fall down.

stilts

This man is a puppeteer. He has lots of puppets. This one is a dragon. There are strings on the puppets. The man pulls the strings and the puppets walk and sit. They look like tiny people and animals.

A reporter is talking to the puppeteer. Let's listen.

Reporter: Did you make your puppets?

Puppeteer: Yes, I made all of them.

Reporter: What did you use?

Puppeteer: I used wood. I always use wood.

Reporter: Why?

Puppeteer: Because I can cut it easily. Look at this puppet. First I made a round head. Next I cut long, thin pieces. They were the arms and legs. Then I cut a fatter, wider piece. That was the body.

Reporter: What did you do next?

Puppeteer: I made the clothes. Then I fixed the strings onto the puppet.

Reporter: What is this puppet?

Puppeteer: He's a boy. His name is Jack. This puppet is bigger. She is Jack's mother. This puppet is the biggest. He is the giant.

Reporter: Are these puppets for *Jack and the beanstalk*?

Puppeteer: That's right. That's the show today. It's starting now.

Reading comprehension and vocabulary

1 **Answer the questions. Write short answers.**

1 How many sticks is the woman juggling with? _____

2 What is at the end of the fire blower's stick? _____

3 Who is the tallest person in the park? _____

4 Where are his stilts? _____

5 What do the puppets look like? _____

6 Why does the puppeteer use wood? _____

7 What is the name of the show today? _____

2 **What are these people? Write the words.**

_____ _____ _____ _____

3 **Complete the sentences.**

1 In the market there are shops and colourful s_____

2 First the juggler throws a stick into the a_____.

3 Then she throws a_____.

4 The fire blower holds a s_____.

5 He blows over a small f_____

6 The stilt walker is the tallest p_____ in the park.

7 There are s_____ on the puppets.

8 The puppeteer makes the head, arms, legs and b_____ from wood.

92

Unit 9 Reading comprehension, vocabulary: literal questions, short answers, gapfill.

Speaking

1 Talk about the picture. Then listen.   **2** Listen and read.

Stop, thief!
Part 3: In the market square

 Where is he?

 He came into this square, I'm sure.

 Oh, look! Musicians!

 She's a very good singer.

 Wow! An acrobat!

 He's walking on his hands!

 We haven't got time to watch him.

 Be careful, Toby! Mind the painter!

 Oops! Sorry!

 Look! There he is!

 Why is he talking to that statue?

 I don't know. Come on!

 Stop!

 Oh! It isn't a statue!

 Why are you following my friend?

 He's got my suitcase. He's a thief!

 No, he isn't. Go away! Go home!

 No, we must catch him.

 Come on! Quick! After him!

Stop!

3 Listen and say.   **4** Talk about the story.   **5** Now you!

Grammar

1 Look!

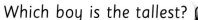 Which boy is the tallest?

 Tom is the tallest.

Jim　　Ben　　Tom

Ask and answer.

1　girl – the shortest ?

Lisa　　Meg　　Anna

2　dog – the smallest ?

Rex　　Mimi　　Fred

3　clown – the saddest ?

Koko　　Miki　　Puku

4　cat – the fattest ?

Tibby　　Poppy　　Minty

2 Look!

 This car is fast.

 This car is faster.

  This car is the fastest.

Point and say.

1　thick

2　big

3　long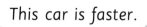

4　happy

Grammar in conversation

1 🔊 **Listen and read.**

What are you doing?

I'm watching a film.

Why?

Because it's good.

Why is it good?

Because it's an exciting story.

What's it about?

A sailor. He sailed across the sea.

Why?

He sailed across the sea because he wanted to find gold.

Why?

Because gold is expensive. And don't ask why!

Why not?

Oh! Go away!

2 🔊 **Listen and say.**

3 Now you!

4 🔊 **Listen and sing.**

What is the wind?
Why does it blow?
Why, why, why? I don't know!
What are the clouds?
Where do they go?
Where, where, where? I don't know!
What makes the rain?
What makes the snow?
So many questions! So much to know!

Listening

1 **Look, listen and point.**

A

B

C

Come back!

D

E

F

2  **Listen again and write the letters.**

1 ☐   2 ☐   3 ☐   4 ☐   5 ☐   6 ☐

3 Tell the story.

Phonics

Look and listen!

oy   boy

Don't annoy the boy, please.
Play with your toy.
Let the boy enjoy his toy, please.
Don't annoy the boy!

→ Now look at WB p87 Use of English

Class composition

1 Look at the picture. Write two sentences about the juggler.

This woman is a juggler.

_____

_____

**2 The reporter is talking to the juggler.
Read her answers. Write the questions.**

_____

I can juggle with five sticks.

_____

No, it's very difficult.

_____

Yes, I can juggle with oranges, too.

_____

No, I can't juggle with bananas!

_____

Yes, I made my clothes.

_____

I work here in the afternoon.

_____

Yes, I like my work. It's fun.

Revision 3

Read. Look at the picture.

The children went to the city yesterday.

What did they see?   What did they hear?   What did they have?

Talk about the picture. What shops were there in the mall? What was in the station?

Project 3

1 **Find out the names of these things. Look on the internet or in a book.**

Write the name. Answer the questions.

The tallest mountain
How tall is it? Where is it?

The longest river
How long is it? Where is it?

The longest bridge
How long is it? Where is it?
Which river does it cross?

The biggest city
Where is it?
How many people live there?

The fastest animal
What is it? How fast can it run?

The biggest fish
What is it? How long is it?

The smallest bird
What is it? How big is it?

2 **Write. Draw pictures or find a pictures on the internet.**

Read out your work.

The tallest mountain is ....

The tallest mountain is ... It is ......metres tall. It is in ....

London sights

A trip on the Thames

Reading 🔵

You can travel through London on the river. The name of the river is the Thames. You can sit on a river boat and see many famous buildings.

Big Ben

You can see this clock tower. Inside the tower there is a heavy metal bell. Its name is Big Ben. Every hour this big bell sounds. It weighs 13,500 kilos. It is heavier than two elephants.

The London Eye

Tower Bridge

River boats go past the London Eye. People ride on this enormous wheel. It turns very slowly. At the top you can see across the city. The London Eye opened in 2000.

Boats go under Tower Bridge. Sometimes tall ships go up the river. A red light stops the traffic. The bridge opens. The ship passes through. The bridge closes again.

You can see this tower. It tells people about the Great Fire of London in 1666. It is 61 metres high. It is 61 metres from the start of the fire. The fire started on Sunday 2nd September in a baker's shop in Pudding Lane. It was two o'clock in the morning and everyone was asleep…

The Monument

Sunday

"Fire! Fire!"

A servant woke up and saw the flames. "Fire, fire!" he shouted. Everyone woke up. They threw water on the fire but it did not stop.

Monday

"Leave your houses!"

The people could not stop the fire. The wind blew and the fire got bigger. It burned other buildings. "Leave your houses!" the mayor said.

Tuesday

Pull down those houses! We must stop the fire.

The fire burned hundreds of houses. It burned the old London Bridge. "Pull down those houses. We must stop the fire," said the king.

Wednesday

Now we are stopping the fire.

They pulled down many houses. The fire could not burn them. The wind did not blow. "Now we are stopping the fire," said the king.

Thursday

What are we going to do?

The fire stopped but thousands of people did not have homes. "What are we going to do?" they asked.

Friday

We are going to build a new city.

The king sent food for the people. He talked to the builders. "We are going to build a new city," he said.

Reading comprehension and vocabulary

1 **Read the statements. Write *true* or *false*.**

1 You can travel through London on the river Thames. ＿＿＿＿＿＿＿
2 Inside the tower there is a clock. ＿＿＿＿＿＿＿
3 River boats go under the London Eye. ＿＿＿＿＿＿＿
4 Tower Bridge opens and ships pass through. ＿＿＿＿＿＿＿
5 The Monument tells people about the Great Tower of London. ＿＿＿＿＿＿＿
6 The fire stopped on Sunday 2nd September, 1666. ＿＿＿＿＿＿＿

Correct the false sentences.

＿＿＿＿＿＿＿＿＿＿＿＿＿＿＿＿＿＿＿＿＿＿＿＿＿＿＿＿＿＿＿＿＿＿＿＿
＿＿＿＿＿＿＿＿＿＿＿＿＿＿＿＿＿＿＿＿＿＿＿＿＿＿＿＿＿＿＿＿＿＿＿＿
＿＿＿＿＿＿＿＿＿＿＿＿＿＿＿＿＿＿＿＿＿＿＿＿＿＿＿＿＿＿＿＿＿＿＿＿
＿＿＿＿＿＿＿＿＿＿＿＿＿＿＿＿＿＿＿＿＿＿＿＿＿＿＿＿＿＿＿＿＿＿＿＿

2 **Who are these people? Write the words.**

servant   mayor   builders   king   baker

＿＿＿＿＿＿＿＿＿＿＿   ＿＿＿＿＿＿＿＿＿＿＿   ＿＿＿＿＿＿＿＿＿＿＿

＿＿＿＿＿＿＿＿＿＿＿   ＿＿＿＿＿＿＿＿＿＿＿

3 **Circle the odd one out.**

1 house   castle   tower   ship   shop

2 builder   brother   baker   painter   carpenter

3 heavy   famous   burn   enormous   huge

Speaking

1 Talk about the picture. 🎧 Then listen. **2** 🎧 Listen and read.

Stop, thief!
Part 4: At the bridge

 Come on! Don't stop!

 But I'm tired.

 Would you like a rest, Molly?

 No, I'm OK.

 He ran down this street, I'm sure.

 Perhaps he's going to cross the river.

 Look! There's the bridge.

 Can you see him?

Yes, there he is. I can see his red hat.

 He's running over the bridge.

 Quick! After him!

 Wait! What's happening?

 Oh, no! There's a red light.

 We must wait.

 A big ship is coming.

 The bridge is opening.

 It's very slow.

 He's running away.

 We're never going to catch him now.

3 🎧 Listen and say. **4** Talk about the story. **5** Now you!

Grammar

1 Look!

The light is red.

The bridge is going to open.

The cars are going to stop.

We're never going to catch the thief.

Read and write the letters.

 A

 B

 C

 D

1 It's going to rain. _____

2 He's going to fall. _____

3 They're going to fly._____

4 I'm going to swim. _____

2 Look!

What is the boy going to do?

He's going to play football.

Ask and answer.

play	run	eat	burn	catch	jump

1

2

3

4

5

6

Grammar in conversation

1  **Listen and read.**

Let's look at the menu.

OK.

I'm going to have a sandwich. Would you like one?

No, thank you, Aunt Jane.

How about a nice salad?

No, thanks.

Well, what would you like?

Can I have a pizza?

Of course! And what would you like to drink?

I'd like orange juice, please.

Are you ready to order, madam?

Yes. We'd like one chicken sandwich, one large pizza, one orange juice and a nice cup of tea.

Thank you, madam.

2 **Listen and say.**

3 **Now you!**

4 **Listen and sing.**

It's the most delicious sandwich in the world!
It's the most delicious sandwich in the world!
Peanut butter and strawberry jam.
Peanut butter and strawberry jam.
It's sticky, it's scrummy,
It's yummy in your tummy.
It's the most delicious sandwich in the world!

Listening

1 🎧 **Listen.**

What is the boy going to make?

Tick the right box.

1

2

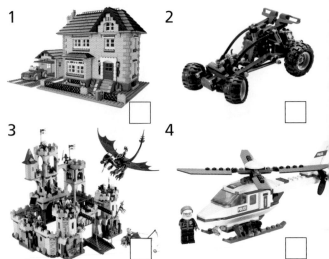

3

4

2 🎧 **Listen again and answer the questions.**

1 Is the building going to be big or small?
2 How many towers is it going to have?
3 What are the windows going to be like?
4 How about the door?
5 What is the boy going to put on the towers?
6 Who is going to live there?

Phonics 🎧 Look and listen!

ur	burn

The wheels turn, the wheels turn,
The nurse is travelling fast.
The fire burns, the fire burns,
The nurse is home at last.

→ Now look at WB p97 Use of English

Class composition

Read and look at the pictures. What happened next? Write the story.

Make the streets wider.

go   old city   talk to builders

_____
_____
_____
_____

Make the buildings taller.

point   picture   new houses

_____
_____
_____
_____

We must not use wood for the new buildings.

builders   look at   old houses

_____
_____
_____
_____

We are going to build stronger houses.

builders   fetch   brick   stone

_____
_____
_____
_____

World festivals

Reading *Festivals in different seasons*

An autumn festival in China

The autumn is harvest time. The moon looks very big. People hang up lanterns and eat round moon cakes.

A winter festival in Japan

There are ice statues and a huge snow building. You can go inside it. Children slide down a giant ice slide. There are coloured lights in the snow.

A spring festival in Spain

People make giant statues. They use paper and wood. They take the statues through the streets. Then they burn them and there are fantastic fireworks.

A summer festival in Scotland Actors and musicians come from all over the world. There are plays every day. They tell new stories and they tell old stories, too.

Do you know the story of Androcles and the lion ? It is a very old story.

There is also an emperor , two soldiers   and a storyteller.

Androcles was a slave. His master was not kind. One day, Androcles ran away.
He ran through the forest for hours and hours. At last he came to a stream.

 Is there any water here? I am very thirsty. I must drink some water.

 Grrr!

 Oh! It's a huge lion. I can't run away. I am very, very tired.

 Grrr owww!

 Oh, you aren't jumping on me, Mr Lion. Why not?

 OWWW!

 What is wrong? Is there something in your paw?

 Ooh! Ooh!

 Oh, look! A big thorn! I can pull it out. Stay still, Mr Lion. …There! It is out.

 Prrrr…prrrr…

 Are you going now? Well, goodbye, Mr Lion.

 The lion went away into the forest. The next day, some soldiers found Androcles. They took him to the emperor.

 Androcles! You ran away. Now you must go and fight a lion.

 Me? Fight a lion? Oh, no. The lion is going to eat me.

 Soldiers! Throw Androcles to the lion.

 Come on, Androcles. Come this way, go through the gate. Goodbye!

 Ooh! There's the lion. It's very big.

 Grr!

 The lion is going to eat Androcles!

 Help. It's coming! Oh, no!

 Hey! look there! The lion is sitting next to Androcles.

 It's holding out its paw.

 What's going on? Bring Androcles and the lion to me. Now!

Reading comprehension and vocabulary

1 Answer the questions.

   1 Where is the autumn festival?

   2 What do people eat in the autumn festival?

   3 What can children do in the winter festival?

   4 Which festival happens in Spain?

   5 What do the people do with the statues?

   6 When is the festival in Scotland?

   7 Where do the actors and musicians come from?

2 What do you think?

   1 Why did Androcles run away from his master?

   2 Why didn't the lion jump on Androcles in the forest?

   3 Why did Androcles take the thorn our of the lion's paw?

   4 Why didn't the lion eat Androcles?

3 Read. Write the season under the correct picture.

In spring people put plants in the ground. Summer is the hottest season.
In autumn people pick fruit. Winter is the coldest season.

1  2  3  4

_____ _____ _____ _____

Speaking

1 Talk about the picture. Then listen.   **2** Listen and read.

Stop, thief!
Part 5: Is that him?

 We're on the other side of the river.

 At last!

 Where's the thief?

 I can't see him.

 I'm never going to get my suitcase now.

 What's this big building?

 It's the Children's Theatre.

 'Summer Festival'.

 Look! There are some photos of the show.

 Are there any famous actors?

 No, there aren't any famous people.

 I don't believe it! Look at that photo!

 It's him! It's the thief!

 Perhaps he's inside the theatre.

 The doors are shut.

 Perhaps there's a door at the back.

 Come on! Let's have a look!

3  Listen and say.   **4** Talk about the story.   **5** Now you!

Grammar

1 Look!

> There is some juice in a jug.

> There are some cakes on a plate.

Read and say *Yes* or *No*.

1 There is some fruit in a basket.
2 There is some water in a bottle.
3 There is some chicken on the table.
4 There are some sandwiches on a plate.
5 There are some grapes in the basket.
6 The girl has got some flowers in her hair.

Talk about the picture.

2 Look!

> Is there any water in the jug?

> Are there any cakes on the plate?

  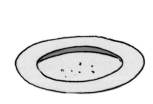 

No, there isn't any water in the jug.

No, there aren't any cakes on the plate.

Ask and answer.

1 juice – jug ?   2 fruit – basket ?   3 water – bottle ?

4 sandwiches – plate ?   5 grapes – basket ?   6 flowers – jug ?

Grammar in conversation

1 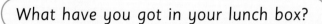 **Listen and read.**

What have you got in your lunch box?

I've got some cheese sandwiches.

Have you got any fruit?
Have you got any grapes?

I've got an apple but
I haven't got any grapes.

What else have you got?

I've got some chocolate
and some little cakes.

Very nice! Lucky you!

What have you got
in your lunchbox?

I left my lunch box at home.

Would you like a sandwich?

Yes, please.

2 Listen and say.

3 Now you!

4 Listen and say.

This is my secret box.
These are my treasures. Come and see!
A golden leaf, a blue-green stone,
A pretty ring, a silver key,
A shark's tooth, a pink shell.
Listen! You can hear the sea!
An eagle's feather, a shiny penny.
These are my treasures. Have you got any?

Listening

1 **Do you remember the story of Androcles and the lion?**

 **Listen and point.**

a

b

c

d

e

f

2  **Listen again and write the letters.**

1 _____   2 _____   3 _____   4 _____   5 _____   6 _____

3 Complete the sentences.

1 Androcles stopped by a _____ because he was tired and _____ .

2 A _____ lion walked towards Androcles. He was very _____ .

3 Androcles pulled a _____ out of the lion's _____ .

🎧 **Listen again and check.**

Phonics 🎧

Look and listen!

| or | morning |  |

Good morning, good morning
It's time for sports.
Please put on your shorts.
It's our morning for sports.

→ Now look at WB p107 Use of English

Class composition

**1 Read what happened next to Androcles and the lion.
Write what Androcles says.**

The soldiers took Androcles and the lion to the emperor.

Why did you run away from your master?

_____

Where did you go?

_____

What happened?

_____

_____

Did the lion jump on you?

_____

What did the lion do?

_____

What was wrong?

_____

What did you do?

_____

My soldiers caught this lion yesterday. Is it the same lion?

_____

The lion did not hurt you because you helped it in the forest.

You are a kind man, Androcles. You can go free and the lion can go too.

_____

Reading

Buildings around the world

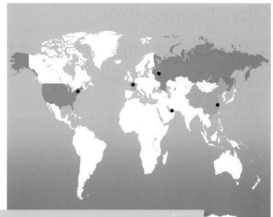

Cities look fantastic at night. In the evening the sun goes down. The sky gets darker and darker. Slowly the bright colours go, too. Everything looks grey.

Then the lights come on. Silver metal shines and the colours are bright again. Cities look different at night. There are glittering lights and dark shadows. The buildings look beautiful.

Paris

This is Paris. It is the biggest city in France. In the middle of it stands a famous tower. It is 300 metres tall and more than 100 years old. It first opened on 6th May 1889. It looks like a tall metal giant. He is standing still in the middle of the city.

Shanghai

This tower is new. It is in Shanghai. Shanghai is a very big city in China. What does the tower look like? A space ship? A strange plant? Parts of the building are round. They look like huge shiny balls.

Moscow

This building is in Moscow. Moscow is the biggest city in Russia. There are nine different towers and they are painted different colours. What do you think it looks like? Lots of giant ice creams? An enormous cake? The colours are bright but this building is more than 450 years old.

New York

This is New York in the United States of America. There are many tall buildings in this city. New York is on an island. These buildings are close to each other. They look like huge glittering rocks standing in the sea.

Dubai

Dubai is a city with many new buildings. It is in the United Arab Emirates. This tall building is a hotel. It opened on 1st December 1999. It looks like a ship's sail. It stands on a very small island next to the beach. It is the only building on the island.

Reading comprehension and vocabulary

1 Read. Circle ending A or B.

1 In the evening the sun   A goes away.   B goes down.

2 Cities look different   A at night.   B in the light.

3 In the middle of Paris there is   A a famous giant.   B a famous tower.

4 The tower in Shanghai is   A new.   B very big.

5 The building in Moscow is over 450   A metres high.   B years old.

6 New York is on   A huge rocks.   B an island.

7 The hotel in Dubai is the only building   A on the island.   B on the beach.

2 Find three words to do with light. Find three words to do with night.

grey	glitter	shadow	night	bright	shine	dark

light   _____   _____   _____

night   _____   _____   _____

3 Where are these buildings? Write the cities.

Dubai	Paris	New York	Moscow	Shanghai

1 _____   2 _____   3 _____   4 _____   5 _____

1 Talk about the picture. Then listen.　**2** Listen and read.

Stop, thief!
Part 6: What's going on?

 You can't run away this time.

 What's going on? Why are you following me?

 Because you've got my suitcase.

 It isn't yours.

 Well, whose suitcase is it?

 It's mine.

 Who are you?

 My name's Alan. I'm an actor.

 What's in that suitcase?

 My costume for the play. Look!

 I don't understand. Where's my suitcase?

♫ Ring-a-ding-a-ding-dong! ♪

 Oh, it's my mobile. Hello? Yes…Yes… OK. Goodbye.

 Who was that?

 Toby's mum. Toby! You left your suitcase at home!

 What? Toby!

 Alan, I'm really, really sorry.

 That's OK. Don't worry! Come and see the play. There are fireworks afterwards.

 Oh, wow! Fantastic! Thanks, Alan!

3 Listen and say.　**4** Talk about the story.　**5** Now you!

Grammar

1 Look!

This shoe is his.

This shoe is yours.

This hat is mine.

This hat is hers.

Mine or *yours*? What are they saying?

1

2

3

4

His or *hers*? Point and say.

1 2  3  4 5  6

2 Look!

These hats are ours.

What are they saying?

These boots are theirs.

1

2

3

4

Grammar in conversation

1 🎧 **Listen and sing.**

January, February, March,
April, May and June,
July, August, September,
October, November, December.
These are the months of the year.
These are the months of the year.

2 🎧 **Listen and read.**

What's the date today?

It's the fifteenth of May.

When's your birthday, Joe?

It's on the ninth of August.

When's your birthday, Helen?

It's on the twenty-second of October.

How about you, Sam?
When's your birthday?

That's today!

It's on the fifteenth of May.

Yes, today's my birthday.

Happy birthday, Sam!

3 🎧 **Listen and say.**

4 **Now you!**

Listening

1 🎧 **Listen and point. Then write the letters.**

1 _____ 2 _____ 3 _____ 4 _____

2 🎧 **Listen again and answer the questions.**

1 What date was it?
2 Was the Tower Restaurant cheap or expensive?
3 How did they go up to the restaurant?
4 Why was Mark scared?
5 What did they have for their dinner?
6 What was Annie's big surprise?

Phonics 🎧

Look and listen!

ow   tower

A cow walks round the tower.
She stops and eats a flower.
A clown with a crown
sits down in the town
and talks to the cow with the flower.

→ Now look at WB p116 Use of English

Class composition

Look at the pictures. Read the words in the box. Write about the building.

Sydney Opera House

This is the _____

Sydney is a very big city. It is in _____

The opera house is _____

_____

_____

_____

_____

_____

_____

Sydney Opera House

Sydney, Australia

67m high,
183m long
120m wide
opened - 20 October 1973

near to - bridge
next to - water
white roofs

It looks like:
butterflies
birds
an insect
flowers
shells

Revision 4

1 🎧 Listen and read.

Next month I am going to visit London. I am going to take some photos of Tower Bridge because I need them for my school project.

Next winter we are going to go to Moscow. I am going to take some thick gloves and a hat because it is going to be very cold.

Next spring we are going to climb a very tall tower in Paris. There is a restaurant near the tower and I'm going to have some lemon ice cream.

Next summer we are going to stay in a big hotel in Dubai. We aren't going to see any camels in the city but we are going to ride camels in the desert.

Next autumn we are going to travel to Shanghai. We are going to see lots of lanterns in the streets because there is a big festival in the autumn.

2 Match the building and the person.

1   2   3   4  5

3 Who is going to...

1   2  3  4   5

eat this?   ride this?   see these?   take these?   wear these?

4 Who is going to travel in these seasons?

5 Who is going to go to...

England?   the United Arab Emirates?   China?   Russia?   France?

Project 4: A visit to a city

1 Choose any city. Find out about it. Look on the internet or in a book.

2 You are going to go to this city. Think about these questions. Use your own ideas for the answers. Write short answers.

What is the name of the city? _____

When are you going to go? _____

How are you going to travel there? _____

Who are you going to travel with? _____

Where are you going to stay? _____

Does a river go through the city? _____

Are there any bridges? _____

Is it by the sea? _____

Are there any castles or towers? _____

What are the buildings like? tall? new? old? interesting? _____

What are the streets like? wide? busy? small? noisy? _____

Can you see other things in the city? _____

What are you going to do in the city? _____

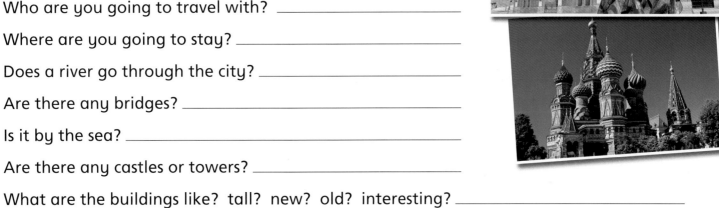

3 Use your answers to write about your visit. Begin like this:

Next ... I am going to go to ... I am going to travel by...

4 Draw pictures of the city or find pictures on the internet.

5 Read out your work.

Word list
(The number is the unit where you can find the word.)

A

above (2)
acrobat (9)
across (2)
actor (9)
address (6)
after (5)
again (1)
ago (4)
air (9)
amazing (6)
America (4)
angry (2)
animal (1)
annoy (9)
another (9)
around (adv) (8)
art (1)
artist (9)
ask (8)
aunt (8)
autumn (11)
axe (4)

B

bad (5)
baker (10)
barn (2)
beans (2)
beanstalk (2)
because (9)
believe (6)
below (2)
belt (3)
board (1)
break (school
  time) (1)
bridge (2)
brilliant (6)
bring (11)
broken (2)
bronze (6)

builder (3)
building (10)
burn (10)
busy (3)

C

café (8)
cage (2)
camera (3)
careful (4)
carpenter (3)
carriage (7)
catch (apprehend) (8)
CD (5)
CD player (5)
centimetre (3)
channel (TV) (4)
cheaper (5)
children (1)
China (11)
choose (4)
city (1)
class (1)
close (v) (10)
close (adj) (12)
cluck (2)
colourful (5)
come back (2)
competition (4)
congratulations (6)
cost (v) (5)
cow (2)
cross (adj) (2)
cross (v) (10)
cry (8)
cup (6)
cycling (6)
cylinder (5)

D

day (11)
dial (5)
different (3)
difficult (1)
digital (5)
dinosaur (7)
dirty (5)
disc (5)
doctor (3)
down (12)
dragon (9)
drop (8)
Dubai (12)
duckling (2)

E

each (9)
each other (6)
earphones (3)
earring (8)
easy (1)
emperor (11)
end (n) (4)
engine (7)
enjoy (9)
enormous (2)
enter (competition) (4)
envelope (6)
escalator (8)
every (10)
everyone (8)
everything (3)
everywhere (2)
exciting (1)
expensive (5)

F

face (n) (5)
fall down (6)
famous (10)
fantastic (2)

D

farm (1)
farmer (2)
favourite (6)
festival (11)
fetch (4)
field (2)
fight (v) (7)
film (5)
find (8)
fire (3)
fire blower (9)
fireman (3)
fireworks (11)
first (adv) (5)
flame (9)
flat (adj) (5)
float (8)
floor (8)
fold (4)
follow (9)
France (12)
fun (2)

G

get (become) (6)
get (receive) (6)
get away (escape) (7)
get to (arrive) (7)
giant (2)
giant (adj) (11)
glittering (12)
goat (2)
gramophone (5)
great (2)
grow (4)
growl (7)
guitar (1)
gymnastics (6)

H

hammer (4)
happen (2)
headset (3)
hear (3)
heavy (10)
helicopter (3)
helmet (3)
hen (2)
high (3)
hole (2)
home (2)
homework (7)
hope (v) (6)
horse (2)
hospital (3)
house (2)
hurry (7)

I

idea (4)
inside (adv) (2)
interesting (1)
international (6)
interview (5)
into (8)
invent (5)
iPod (5)

J

Japan (11)
jar (1)
jeans (7)
joy (9)
judo (6)
juggler (9)

K

keep (4)
kiosk (7)
know (1)

L

lantern (11)
late (1)
learn (1)
leave (go) (10)
leave (not take) (6)
left (dir.) (8)
left (leave) (8)
letter (6)
lesson (1)
lifeguard (3)
lift (v) (4)
lift (n) (elevator) (8)
like (adv) (7)
look like (12)
lose (8)
luck (6)
luggage (7)

M

machine (5)
mall (8)
maths (1)
mayor (10)
medal (6)
metal (4)
metre (3)
microphone (3)
mind out (9)
mirror (8)
missing (adj) (8)
mobile phone (5)
money (2)
Moscow (12)
mountain (3)
music (1)
musician (9)
must (7)

n

nails (4)
near (4)
need (4)
nest (2)
New York (12)
next (5)
now (1)
nurse (3)

O

only (5)
other (10)
outside (8)

P

page (1)
painter (3)
paper (4)
Paris (12)
Pass (v) (10)
passengers (7)
passes (10)
past (adv) (8)
paw (11)
pay (3)
perhaps (4)
person (9)
phonograph (5)
pick up (2)
piece (4)
pilot (3)
pioneer (4)
pipes (3)
place (n) (5)
plant (1)
plastic (4)
platform (7)
pleased (2)
plumber (3)
pocket (3)
polite (7)
poor (money) (2)

pot (4)

pot (4)
prize (6)
programme (TV) (4)
protect (3)
pull down (10)
puppet (9)
puppeteer (9)
purse (10)
put (4)

R

rap (song) (5)
ready (7)
really (adv) (5)
record (v) (5)
remember (6)
rest (in repose) (10)
rich (3)
right (dir) (8)
road (8)
roar (v) (2)
roof (2)
rope (4)
round (adv) (5)
round (prep) (8)
rule (regs) (7)
run away (11)
rush (v) (7)
Russia (6)

S

sailing (6)
same (adj) (11)
save (rescue) (1)
saw (tool) (4)
say (3)
scarf (8)
school (1)
science (1)
scissors (3)
Scotland (11)
screen (5)
season (11)
sell (2)

send (6)
servant (10)
shadow (12)
Shanghai (12)
sheep (2)
shoe shop (8)
shout (7)
show (v) (2)
show (n) (9)
show jumping (6)
shut (adj) (11)
silly (5)
singer (5)
skiing (6)
skip (4)
skittles (4)
slam (7)
slave (11)
sob (8)
soldier (11)
some (6)
son (2)
song (5)
sound (v) (2)
Spain (11)
speak (3)
special (2)
spend (money) (8)
sports (1)
spring (season) (11)
square (built env.) (9)
stable (2)
stall (market) (9)
start (v) (10)
statue (9)
stay (3)
stick (n) (9)
sticky tape (4)
stilt walker (9)
stop (7)
strange (7)
stream (11)
string (4)
suddenly (8)

suitcase (7)
sum (1)
summer (11)
supermarket (8)
sure (9)
surprised (2)
swan (2)

T

take (2)
tear (n) (8)
tell (4)
terrible (2)
theatre (11)
thief (7)
thing (3)
thorn (11)
thousand (10)
ticket (7)
ticket office (7)
time (2)
timetable (1)
together (5)
too (6)
top (2)
tower (2)
town (12)
track (6)
tractor (2)
traffic (10)
tram (7)
travel (4)
trolley (7)
turn (v) (5)

U

uncle (8)
uniform (3)
United Arab Emirates (12)
United States of America (12)

V

video (v) (5)
video camera (5)
visit (1)
visitor (4)
voice (5)

W

wait (8)
want (1)
watch (n) (3)
weekend (2)
weigh (10)
well (adj) (6)
whistle (n) (7)
why (9)
wide (3)
win (6)
winter (11)
woman (3)
wood (mat.) (4)
wool (4)
word (4)
work (n) (v) (3)
world (6)
worried (3)

Y

year (4)